Murphy the Ten visits the US Open

Want to play??

Written by
MAURA MOYNIHAN

Ilustrated by
NINA LARKIN MATEYUNAS

 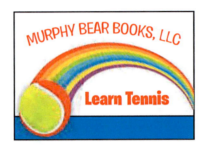 

To Erin, Gavan, Connor, Dillon MM
To Christopher, Keira, Nina NLM

Special Thanks: USTA, Arthur Ashe Kids' Day, JC11, Dr. & Mrs Gavan Moynihan,
Ireland's Marguerite Murphy of Sandycove, Vito Stelino & Dave Moseley

Copyright © 2011 by Maura Moynihan
Copyright © 2011 illustrated by Nina Larkin Mateyumas

Book Design by Michael Wilson 2013

All rights reserved. Printed in the United States of America
www.Murphybearbooks.blogspot.com   www.FirstRacquet.org

Library of Congress Cataloging-in-Publication Data
Murphy the Tennis Bear visits the US Open by Maura Moynihan-Second edition 2014
Summary: Murphy Bear & Gavan Gator visit Arthur Ashe Kids' Day US Open NYC, tennis tips follow.
ISBN: 978-0-578-08550-0 (paperback)
Tennis - Juvenille literature

For further information contact Murphy Bear Books LLC at murphybearbooks@aol.com

Murphy Bear Books, LLC is dedicated to inspiring in children an appreciation for tennis and nature that will keep them healthy and fit for life.
"Feel encouraged, you are on the road to more and more progress"

The train pulled in. Late summer breezes danced over the platform. Parrots shined like emeralds in a morning haze. It was Murphy's first visit to New York City.

"Nothing looks like Florida," he thought. . . . "Except for the sky."

"Hurry!" his friend said. "We're at the greatest tennis tournament in the world."

Lining up, Gavan Gator asked Murphy about his nickname.
"I play lots of tennis and I eat healthy," he explained.
"So my dad calls me MurphFit."
"Fitness is Energy!" Gavan replied, with a high five.
And a power glowed from their hands.

"Welcome to Arthur Ashe Kids' Day!" said the royal blue crew. In a silver mist, the giant stadium towered like a spaceship. Music and laughter boomed.

Inside the smaller stadium, stars were practicing. Fans from around the globe cheered, as tennis balls exploded. Murphy grabbed his camera. Then he saw someone waving. It was Erin Bear with her face painted.

"I didn't know you were coming here!" she marveled.
"I'm going to the Fan Experience, follow me....
Wait, let's ask a volunteer to take our picture."
"Say TENNIS," Kyoka Kat beamed.

Murphy felt a thud. Astounded, they froze like statues. "Where on earth did you come from?" Kyoko asked. The parrot squawked softly. They burst into laughter and it whizzed away.

Then he tossed the balls in the air. "They bounce lower and move slower," Chen explained. "The colors are marked for your age. Some are foam and others are fuzzy felt."

Murphy squished a ball before the *rally*. He daydreamed about a live sponge under the sea. "Pay attention," Gavan grumbled. "*Drop hit*." "WOOSH" came off Murphy's strings then he heard "PING."

"*Overhead smashes*," Chen instructed.
"Stand sideways, point to the ball and SMASH." Erin's flew like a home run. Gavan sliced wide. Murphy caught air. . . . But with practice, they were aiming on the court like darts to the bull's eye.

Outside, marshmallow clouds hung low. Flowers swayed in the breeze. Zig-zagging by jugglers and stilt men, a scrumptious scent stirred their bellies. They stopped at the Food Village for tomato soup, brown bread and chocolate cherries.

Arriving at the Storyteller, rain misted over the grounds. Miss Angel's hands swirled with her smile. Her eyes moved like the ocean.

She held up a nest. . . .
In an instant, the curious parrot landed.
Astonished. . . .
she tumbled off her chair. Everyone laughed, and so did she!

Murphy saw Erin taking pictures. Sunbursts created a rainbow. "Look up," Miss Angel announced. "See that arch? It's the path a tennis ball makes as it soars up and over the net. Let's pretend to hit a *topspin rainbow ball* with a *groundstroke*."

"Where did Erin go?" Gavan groaned. Murphy pointed to the US Open Bookstore. "Look," she shouted. "I bought the book written by the Storyteller. Can you get a picture of us when she signs it?"
"I need my camera back first," Murphy insisted.

Erin looked all around. "OH NO . . . . I just had it."

"We have to find it," he demanded. "I promised my dad I would take pictures."

"Where did you have it last?" Gavan asked.

Murphy used his brain and they ran after him.

But it was nowhere. Alas, they rested.
"Your name and address are on the camera," Gavan reminded him.
"I'm not giving up," he said, sadly.

"Have faith," Gavan pressed. "We can't miss the big show!"
"Or the tennis stars!" Erin added.
Murphy recited his secret prayer. . . . Then he nudged his friends to go.

On the top level of Arthur Ashe Stadium, they gazed over the USTA Billie Jean King National Tennis Center.
"That's the World's Fair Unisphere!" Gavan said.

Murphy's arms flew open.
"Look at the New York City skyline!"
"WOW!" they yelled.
"Hurry, the show is starting!"

Junior players challenged the tennis heroes. They had hummingbird speed.
I wish I could play like them," Erin whispered to Gavan.
"Dedication," he shouted, over the roar of spirited fans.
Next, a champion wheelchair player hit every target. Murphy felt inspired.

Suddenly, the stage lit up. A banner band shook the stadium. On a big TV screen they watched Kyoko and Chen dance. Then it switched to Murphy playing his favorite instument. They sang till the show's end.

Erin was off to Times Square. Gavan bought souvenirs and they wore them on the train. Murphy was happy to be going fishing with his Uncle on Long Island. . . . He wasn't ready to tell his dad about the lost camera.

A few days later, Dad greeted Murphy at the Florida Airport. After big bear hugs, Dad handed him a package.

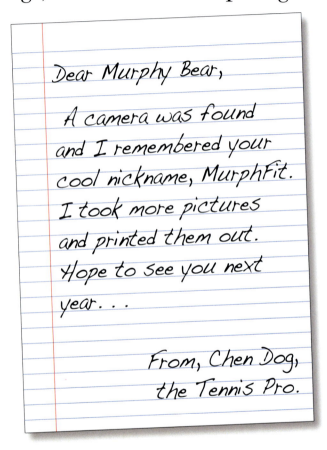

Dear Murphy Bear,

A camera was found and I remembered your cool nickname, MurphFit. I took more pictures and printed them out. Hope to see you next year...

From, Chen Dog, the Tennis Pro.

"A miracle," Murphy gasped. He immediately called his friends. "I have a surprise! I'm the storyteller at my house tomorrow. You're all invited, bring your racquets."

That afternoon, family and friends listened to Murphy's story. . . .
All of a sudden, a tapping noise interrupted them.
"Those parrots were at the US Open!" the kids hollered.
"No way," Dad replied. "In New York City?". . . "Extraordinary!"
"Millions of trees too," Gavan added.

. . . . The proof came from the pictures.

After dinner, Dad set up a portable tennis net on the driveway. Mom and friends *warmed up with yoga*. Radiant rays dipped into the sea. . . . Energy powered from their racquets. On went the lights.

Murphy felt like a star. "US Open at home!" he joked. And they all played tennis till bed time.

Murphy Bear's Tennis Talk

Can you find the *Italicized* words in the story? Their meanings are listed below.

Ace	When a good serve is untouched by the receiver.
Cross Court	A shot that crosses over the net's center.
Doubles	Four players using the full court. Singles is two players not using the doubles alleys.
Down the Alley	A shot in doubles play where the ball is placed down the alley to try to pass the opponent.
Drop Hit	A forehand or backhand shot that starts a rally. Can be practiced against a backboard.
Drop Shot	The stroke after the ball bounces. It's hit with slice and should land close to the net.
Groundstroke	The shot when a player hits the ball after the bounce. It's either a forehand or backhand.
Line	If the tennis ball lands on any part of the line, the shot is good.
Lob	The shot when the ball is hit high into the air.
Overhead Smash	A shot used to return the lob. It's hit above the head with a swing and follow –through.
Racquet Spin	Is to see who serves first. This is like a coin toss. The butt of a racquet has a mark. The spinner calls up or down. Whoever gets the call can choose the serve or the side to start a match.
Rainbow Ball	Author's idea; due to the fact that when the ball is hit with topspin it creates an arch like a rainbow.
Rally	A sequence of shots within a point. Can occur for practicing strokes.
Serve	The overhead shot that starts every point. It must land inside the opponent's service box.
Shake hands	Players do this after a match for good sportsmanship.
Slice	The backspin a ball takes by stroking high to low. The ball usually crosses the net low and lands low.
Topspin	The spin a ball takes after it is brushed with a low to high swing and it forms an arch over the net.
Warm up	One way is Yoga; postures & breath awareness that increases strength, flexibility and concentration.

Gavan Gator's Tennis Tip – Burn that serve, not your skin. Wear your hat and sun block 50+

NATURE NEWS

The Monk or Quaker Parakeets are also named, Brooklyn Parrots. These intelligent, non aggressive birds are a true gift of nature. They coexist well with other native birds. And they just won't give up, even when the deck is stacked against them. They did not fly up to NYC from Argentina on their own. It is believed that in the late 1960's they were supposed to be sold to pet shops in New York. But the parrots were accidently released from their crates at Kennedy Airport, NY. They escaped into the Brooklyn area and now are seen in other parts of NYC.

Million Trees NYC A program to plant and care for one million new trees in the five boroughs of NYC.

US OPEN TRIVIA

Arthur Ashe An African American tennis star who was one of the most prominent players of his time. He won three Grand Slam titles and is the co founders of the NJTL.
Arthur Ashe Kids' Day The pre US Open celebration in memory of Arthur Ashe and to benefit the NJTL. It is filled with fun entertainment, tennis playing, contests, games, live music, tennis stars, and more.
Avenue of the Aces Located on the grounds of the National Tennis Center. It forms a brick pathway. One can buy a brick paver with your name on it and all proceeds go to USTA Serves.
Fan Experience A place for family fun with various games, contests and kid size tennis courts.
NJTL National Junior Tennis & Learning is a USTA nationwide organization seeking to develop the character of young people through tennis.
USTA Is not-for-profit and it's the largest tennis organization in the world.
US Open Held annually in NY in August and September over a two week period. It is the largest attended sporting event in the world. The main tournament consists of five different event championships; men's and women's singles and doubles and mixed doubles. It also has tournaments for senior, junior and wheelchair players. The US Open has been the fourth and final tennis Grand Slam each year.
USTA Serves The national charitable foundation of the USTA.
USTA Billie Jean King National Tennis Center, Flushing Meadows Corona Park in Queens New York City is the largest public tennis facility in the world. It is operated by the USTA for the city of New York.
World's Fair 1964/65 was held on the site of Flushing Meadows Corona Park. The fair's theme was "Peace through Understanding". The theme was symbolized by a twelve story high stainless steel model of the earth called the "Unisphere" which stands on the park today.

USTA STANDARDS

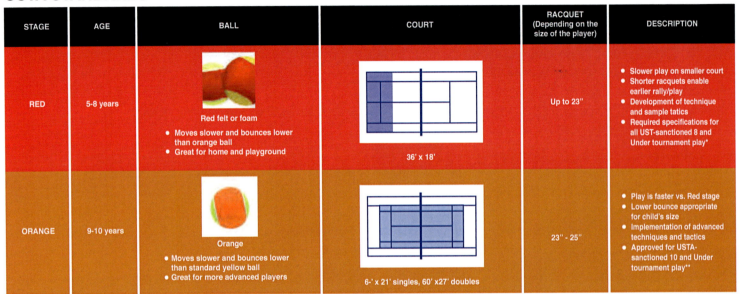

Find a tennis game near you by going to: www.youthtennis.com

	Serve	Rally	Score
Age 5-6	Parent/coach toss or drop hit with red ball	Passing, rolling or tossing red ball	Cooperative rallies
Age 7-8	Overhand serve, Underhand serve or drophit with red ball	Hitting red ball over "net"	2 out of 3 7 point tie break
Ages 9-10	Overhand serve with orange ball	Hitting orange ball over " net"	2 out of 3-4 game sets 3rd set, 7 point tie break

Hitting balls against a wall or garage door is a great way to practice. Just drop hit and swing a forehand or backhand. The red and orange balls are slower so when it bounces back it allows a child to recover and prepare for the next shot. Move closer to the wall and hit volleys before the ball bounces. Always keep those feet on fire!